Piano Sketches

Vitalij Neugasimov

Book 1

18 easy pieces for solo piano

MUSIC DEPARTMENT

OXFORD
UNIVERSITY PRESS

OXFORD
UNIVERSITY PRESS

Great Clarendon Street, Oxford OX2 6DP,
United Kingdom

Oxford University Press is a department of the University of Oxford.
It furthers the University's objective of excellence in research, scholarship,
and education by publishing worldwide. Oxford is a registered trade mark of
Oxford University Press in the UK and in certain other countries

First published 2016

Impression: 6

ISBN 978-0-19-341327-6

Music and text origination by Katie Johnston

Printed in Great Britain on acid-free paper by
Halstan & Co. Ltd, Amersham, Bucks.

Pieces from this collection originally published as part of
Pianoheads Collection 1 and *2* (2009 and 2010)

Contents

Frog Boogie	4
The Mouse and the Elephant	6
Lullaby	8
Blues for Lucy	9
Waltz-Caprice	10
Lazy Bear	12
Birthday March	13
Butterfly	14
Oriental Dance	16
Ballad for Robin Hood	17
Greetings from Cuba	18
Old Scottish Dance	20
Let's Rock	22
Moody Gigue	24
An Idyll	25
Toccata	26
Meditation	28
Walking Around	30

Composer's Note

Welcome to this short series of piano miniatures covering a broad spectrum of musical styles and gestures. Accessible yet engaging, the pieces should appeal melodically and harmonically to developing pianists, and provide opportunities for exploring musical textures and narrative while addressing technical points. They are written for player and listener alike, and hopefully inspire a sense of creativity and wonder at the palette of sound that is available to us.

This collection is dedicated to the memory of my beloved father, Vasilij Neugasimov. The pieces were inspired by my sister Liudmila Neugasimova, an outstanding piano teacher with over 20 years' experience; her encouragement and contribution were immense. I should like to thank, also, Martynas Vilkelis, who helped me to achieve my goal.

Frog Boogie

Vitalij Neugasimov

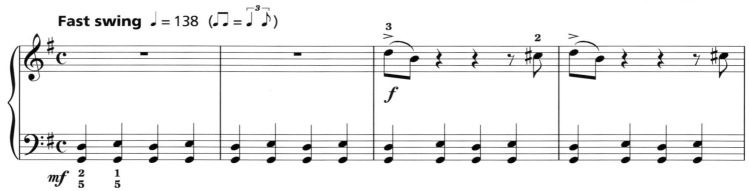

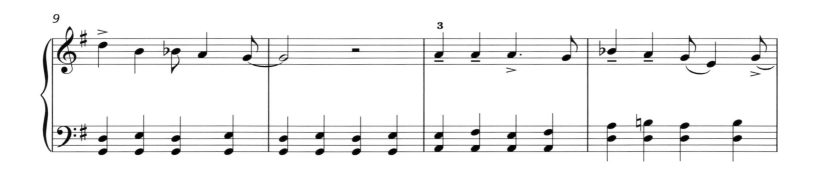

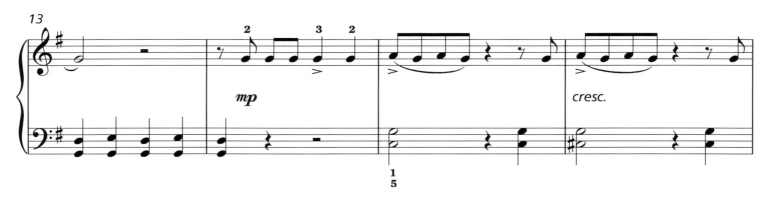

The Mouse and the Elephant

Vitalij Neugasimov

Lullaby

Vitalij Neugasimov

to my sister Liudmila

Blues for Lucy

Vitalij Neugasimov

Waltz-Caprice

Vitalij Neugasimov

Lazy Bear

Vitalij Neugasimov

* Play the repeat on the D.C.

Birthday March

Vitalij Neugasimov

Butterfly

Vitalij Neugasimov

Oriental Dance

Vitalij Neugasimov

* Play the repeat on the D.C.

Ballad for Robin Hood

Vitalij Neugasimov

* All chords may be played *arpeggiato*.

Greetings from Cuba

Vitalij Neugasimov

Old Scottish Dance

Vitalij Neugasimov

Let's Rock

Vitalij Neugasimov

Moody Gigue

Vitalij Neugasimov

An Idyll

Vitalij Neugasimov

Toccata

Vitalij Neugasimov

Giocoso ♩ = 88

Meditation

Vitalij Neugasimov

Walking Around

Vitalij Neugasimov